Russell Davies

Do Interesting

Notice. Collect. Share.

BooK Co

To Mum and Dad

Published by
The Do Book Company 2023
Works in Progress Publishing Ltd
thedobook.co

Text © Russell Davies 2023
Photography © named individuals 2023

10 9 8 7 6 5 4 3 2

To find out more about our company,
books and authors, please visit
thedobook.co or follow us **@dobookco**

5 per cent of our proceeds from the sale
of this book is given to The DO Lectures
to help it achieve its aim of making
positive change: thedolectures.com

Cover designed by James Victore
Book designed and set by Ratiotype

Printed and bound by OZGraf Print
on Munken, an FSC® certified paper

A CIP catalogue record for this book is
available from the British Library

ISBN 978-1-914168-20-8

Contents

Introduction   7

1   **Noticing**   23
2   **Collecting**   55
3   **Sharing**   89

Resources   129
About the author   130
Thanks   131

Pay attention.
Be astonished.
Tell about it.

Mary Oliver

INTRODUCTION

Mary Oliver's words are a pretty good introduction to this book. It has a simple premise.

You can make your work — and the world — more interesting by practising three things:

— **Noticing** — if you pay more attention to the world, it starts to look more interesting

— **Collecting** — if you bang together the things you've noticed, they get more interesting again

— **Sharing** — if you get good at sharing all that stuff with people, it gets even better

This book might help if:

— You have one of those jobs that involve lots of presentations or writing and you work with 'ideas' a lot.

— You don't do any of that just yet, but one day you'd like to do more of that kind of thing.

— You've got a creative project bubbling inside somewhere, you just don't know quite where to start.

Noticing, collecting and sharing will make things more creative, rewarding and fun for you and your colleagues, customers and community (and friends, postal workers, etc).

Scattered within you'll find 34 little habits or exercises. I bet you're already doing some of them; a lot of them are pretty obvious. But sometimes you just need a nudge or reminder to get started.

The three main ones are:

— **Write down things you notice**

— **Get a scrapbook**

— **Start a blog**

It's not that surprising a list, is it? But are you doing these things? If so, fabulous, you'll love this book because it'll be one big pat on the back. If not, well, hopefully we'll get you doing them. They might be obvious, but they work.

There are also some fun side quests you can try. If you don't like some of them, then just pick a few of the others. It's pretty easy, like falling off a log. But onto a gentle bed of moss, dotted with daisies and perfumed with heather.

Don't worry if you don't think of yourself as 'creative'

It is easy for that to feel like a thing other people do. The ones over there with paint on their shirts and a faraway look in their eyes.

It feels like a grand title to ascribe to yourself, a tall order without a painting or novel to show for it. This is all rather silly. Creativity is a defining characteristic of being human. Coming up with ideas, making connections between things, having an imagination... this is all standard Homo sapiens stuff. You are already an ordinary, undistinguished, run-of-the-mill, really creative human being. Just like everybody else.

This is a tasting menu of exercises that will bring that out. A large wooden board bearing some delicious tasty possibilities. Pick the ones that resonate with you and give them a go.

Spit the others out like they contain an unexpected olive.

More probable magic

There are two schools of thought when it comes to creativity:

1. It's a magical, intuitive, mysterious process that can't be forced. You just have to wait for the muse to strike you. It might help if you sip absinthe or are French.

Or:

2. Inspiration is for amateurs. It's a job like any other.
You just need to show up and do the work. Put the hours in. Develop the habits. Churn it out.

This book leans towards the latter view because it's more optimistic. You're not just waiting on fate.

And because sometimes you just want someone to tell you what to do. When the toilet's backing up and there's sewage all over the bathroom, you don't want someone explaining the intricacies of fluid dynamics, you want to know where to stick the plunger.

So this is a pretty didactic book. It'll say *Do This* and *Do That*.

Some people will scoff at that and tell you that human creativity involves something mysterious and ineffable we can't deliberately access.

That's true. We can't *make* ideas happen.

But we can make them much more likely, we can make the magic more probable. That's what we're doing here.

That means making a bit of an effort. Not as much as you might think. But some effort. Some energy.

The people you'll meet in this book might seem like wildly different 'creative types'. Trust me, they're not. They have the same doubts and imposter syndrome as you. They're also convinced they'll never have another interesting idea. But they've learned to make these little efforts. To try these things. To develop these habits.

It's like making pancakes on Shrove Tuesday. You probably haven't made a pancake for a year, so to get a good pancake, you have to make more than one. You have to practise. No one's first pancake is great. You have to try again.

There'll be stuff in here that you'll try and it won't seem very rewarding. Just try it again. And maybe a third or fourth time. The fourth pancake will be golden.

I'm telling you this so you can't say you've not been warned. But the fact that you're reading this suggests you're willing to put in the appropriate amount of work. We're not talking about the effort required to self-build a house or start keeping bees. It's more akin to starting a small, gentle hobby.

But it's not nothing.

The best way to manage that effort is to get yourself some habits.

First forget inspiration. Habit is more dependable. Habit will sustain you whether you're inspired or not.

Octavia E. Butler

Listen to Octavia Butler. If you're ever going to do something vaguely creative (and that's what I'm talking about here, things that are vaguely creative) then you'll need to develop some habits.

Ideas mostly come from the slow, quiet accumulation of seemingly banal and obvious habits. It's just doing the right things to make sure your mind and your life are brimming with hearty compost.

If, occasionally, you have a moment of magic, that will be why. Because of the habits. And you don't have to do them every day. Just dailyish.*

Don't make a religion of these habits. Don't worry about maintaining a streak. That'll just cause despair and abandonment when one day you inevitably fail.

Just fit them in with your life. You don't need to worry about your creative rituals on the day you give birth.

* The idea of dailyishness came from Dan Harris's podcast about meditation.

Why interesting?

I've been circling the idea of 'interestingness' for the last 30 years.

In 1996 I was working as an advertising strategist for the world's best advertising agency. They were famous because they came up with 'Just Do It' and did a bunch of great advertising for Nike.

But I didn't work on Nike. I worked on Microsoft, and the advertising we made sucked.

One of my fellow strategists on Microsoft was a very smart chap called Jeffre Jackson. We spent long hours trying to work out what it was about Nike ads that made them so good and how we could persuade Microsoft to do the same thing.

He kept invoking a 1960s ad man called Howard Gossage. Gossage made unconventional, humane and genuinely funny advertising when that was very rare, and one of the things Jeffre kept quoting was this:

Nobody reads advertising. People read what interests them, and sometimes it's an ad.

If you don't work in advertising, this might seem an unremarkable statement. Inside advertising it was almost heresy. Most of the marketing world had convinced itself that it could bombard audiences with sales messages and force them into consumer compliance through sheer repetition and exposure. Most of the industry still thinks this way.

Nike, through wilfulness and great instincts, had intuited a different way forward. They just tried to make ads that were more 'worth watching' than anything else that could be watched at the same time.

And now Jeffre and I were trying to reverse-engineer what made something 'worth watching' and turn it into a rational programme of communications we could sell to Microsoft.

We never really managed it.

But it put us on paths to 'interestingness'. Jeffre is now more expert and thoughtful than anyone I know about what makes an organisation or its communications interesting. He's writing his own book about it and I urge you to buy it. We'll meet him again later.

How to be interested

A few years later, I was invited to go to the University of Oregon and teach the advertising students something.

Since they were all writers and art directors and I wasn't, I was a bit stumped about what I could tell them. So I tried to consider what might be more generally useful to them in their careers. And thinking about Jeffre and all the most inspiring people I'd come across, I settled on 'How To Be Interesting'.

'Do these specific things', I wanted to say, 'and you will be interesting.'

It sort of worked, so I wrote it up as a blog post. And since it was the early days of blogging, it went modestly viral and I became a minor expert on interestingness. That original blog post is still there. It's dated, but I stick by the opening thoughts I wrote back then:

The way to be interesting is to be interested. You've got to find what's interesting in everything, you've got to be good at noticing things, you've got to be good at listening. If you find people (and things) interesting, they'll find you interesting.

Interesting people are good at sharing. You can't be interested in someone who won't tell you anything. Being good at sharing is not the same as talking and talking and talking. It means you share your ideas, you let people play with them and you're good at talking about them without having to talk about yourself.

I've pursued these kinds of habits myself and I think they've helped me. I've not had a very linear career but it's been, well, interesting.

As far as I'm aware, I'm the only person who's won the top award for advertising strategy (APG Gold) and advertising creativity (D&AD Black Pencil). I've done PowerPoint in the Number 10 cabinet meeting room. I've written years' worth of weekly and monthly columns for famous magazines. I led the marketing team for the fastest growing company in Europe. I've written two books: one about PowerPoint, one about cafés. I've had my art shown in the Royal Academy's Summer Exhibition (with my friend Ben). I've had my sound art transmitted to the whole of Edinburgh. My family have featured on the front of the *Visit Wales* brochure. I started a walking football team. *Vanity Fair* magazine wrote about a 'salon' I hosted which led to a new art movement (it was really just some people having breakfast). I've made programmes for Radio 4, I've won a prize for blogging and I've written a Dimbleby Lecture.

And I started a series of conferences called Interesting. Short talks by enthusiasts about interesting things. They've been happening all over the world now for more than 15 years. Hundreds of people have spoken, thousands have been interested. It's made me realise that there's something pure and fun and magical about just asking, 'What do you find interesting?'

But I've always found 'How To Be Interesting' an awkward way of framing things. It's pretty arrogant. It's like saying I can tell you how to be beautiful.

People have asked me to talk about it and I've done occasional workshops but I always do them sheepishly. I sail past the opening slide and say, 'The secret to being interesting is being interested,' and then just ignore it. But in writing this book I've realised that's not really what I mean.

I was interviewing Tom Whitwell. You'll meet him later. He's an objectively interesting man. He invents strange electronic musical instruments. He writes fascinating lists on the internet. Professionally, he helps businesses solve big complex business problems. And when we talked, he said that the best people at that job are always the ones that can get interested in any problem, no matter how tedious it seems on the surface. They don't get drawn to the obviously cool problems — sport, tech, fashion, purpose — they get stuck into things that seem a bit boring — insurance, infrastructure, finance, logistics — and they find what's interesting about them.

This sparked with me. That's what I've done my whole career. I've ended up doing interesting projects because I can see the possibilities in stuff no one else wants to do. And then, if you do the job properly, you make it interesting to other people.

So that's the 'interestingness' of this book.

It's not about making yourself interesting. It's about making the world interesting. And that means developing skills and habits around ideas, creativity and communication.

It's a tiny superpower. It gives you a lift. And it's a tiny spice. It makes everything tastier.

I saw this and thought of you

And it's not a solo activity.

There are bits you can do on your own. And you have to bring yourself to it. But the best, most interesting ideas and possibilities emerge from conversation and exchange. From planting seeds in other people's soil.

The fashion writer Navaz Batliwalla told me she has a constant back and forth with a friend of hers on Instagram. They're always sharing images with each other, exploring and debating what they find. She describes it as 'I saw this and thought of you'. You probably do something similar.

So when I started writing this book, I realised I needed help. Books are always a collective endeavour, it's just that the teamwork is normally buried in the acknowledgements. Not this time.

There are multiple brains in here. Sometimes it's quotes and ideas I've scavenged along the way. Sometimes mini-interviews with people I've found inspiring. (Full disclosure, some of those people are my friends.) As the Borussia Dortmund footballer Jamie Jermaine Bynoe-Gittens once said, 'You've got to take stuff from other people to make the best version of yourself.'

And I've rounded up a gang to actually help write the thing.

I love them all for their ability to find what's interesting in just about anything.

Anne Shewring has worked in charities most of her life, raising money and spending it effectively. She knows how to communicate and persuade. She's also a funny and gifted writer who's always inventing new ways to tell stories. (Spoiler alert: we're married to each other).

Ben Terrett is a designer who started off doing graphics for canteens and has ended up transforming governments. He's now the CEO of an enormously influential digital transformation consultancy. We've worked together on and off for years. (He's one of my best friends).

Clem Hobson started as a 'brand person' and is now MD of a new kind of property business. She's the ultimate creative generalist, as comfortable with a spreadsheet as she is with a mood board. We've worked together a lot. (She's also one of my best friends).

Denise Wilton started off doing design when that was a thing you did with paper, pens and scalpels. Then she helped to invent how digital things exist at places like b3ta and *moo.com*. She also knits gorgeous tiny animals, makes extraordinary pixel art and writes like a dream. We've worked together a lot too. (Yes, another of my best friends).

You will see me mention individual things they've written as we go. But they also did a lot of work on the main text. There's more than one 'I' in here. And everything we've written is the product of years of conversation. Except for all the mistakes and bad jokes. They're all me.

PART 1

NOTICING

Do stuff.
Be clenched, curious.
Not waiting for
inspiration's shove
or society's kiss
on your forehead.
Pay attention.
It's all about
paying attention.
Attention is vitality.
It connects you
with others.
It makes you eager.
Stay eager.

Susan Sontag

Don't hunt for diamonds — get fascinated by pebbles

The world is already more interesting than anyone can possibly imagine. You just need to pay attention.

That doesn't mean transforming into some kind of hippy loon. You don't have to skip around singing 'hullo clouds, hullo sky'. Neither do you need to be undiscriminating. This is not about pretending that everything is great.

It just means developing some habits that will help you tune in rather than out. And not randomly, not like a gigantic hoover sucking up everything in its path, but in a way that reflects your peculiarities and interests. Tuning the world so you see things that no one else does.

You are already good at this

You already notice stuff that other people don't.

Something in your life has nudged you in a particular direction and you already have a valuable and different perspective.

I'm here to help you find out what it is and encourage you to share it.

The French have a term: *déformation professionnelle*. It's the way your profession influences the way you see the world.

Clem's mum Jamanda, for instance, is a radiologist. She looks at a lot of X-rays and scans and tries to see if there's anything wrong. In a scan, there is a regular appearance and an irregular appearance for all the things she might be looking at. Things like kidneys or spleens. A radiologist is very attuned to any irregularity. A blob. The wrong shade of grey. A curve on a line that shouldn't be there. Anything that is not standard, regular and 'as it should be' is immediately obvious. This changes how Jamanda sees the world. She spots the smallest speck of fluff on the blue carpet running up the stairs. She knows when something has changed in a room. Her pet peeve is aiming for alignment and missing — two pictures hung at slightly different heights. Recently, a slide was presented at work with complete disregard for symmetry. 'I almost can't look at it,' Jamanda complained.

Every job has these little insights, quirks and oddities.

And if it's not in your job, it'll be in your hobbies, or your history or your outlook.

Don't hide your interestingness under a bush. Let us in.

The good news is that starting to notice things isn't like starting most new hobbies, or even most new habits. You don't need to wait to get the proper gym kit, knitting needles or the right kind of flour. If you're lucky, you've already got what you need: the ability to notice the sights, smells, sounds and feel of things around you.

You don't need to be anywhere in particular and you don't need the perfect notebook. To be honest, you don't even need to go outside, although you might prefer it. It's up to you.

Different things happen when you start paying more attention.

You might learn something new, be surprised or delighted. Or perhaps the thing you've noticed will spark a new idea. Sometimes you'll spot something remarkable (not life-changing — that's different), in other words, something worth remarking on, when you're talking to a friend or someone you work with.

And occasionally you'll spot something beautiful. Maybe you'll share that too, or maybe not. There's a certain magic in collecting your own set of secrets about the world.

Sometimes you won't know what you've noticed until you write it down. It's like pulling at a thread. It's not always the noticing that's the thing. It's the thinking that happens when you write about it.

Fall in love with a tree

In 2021 Rachel Syme interviewed the singer Lucy Dacus for *The New Yorker*. Dacus described a game she played when she was a child. It was called 'Fall in Love with a Tree'.

The first tree you see in the distance, you just look at it and notice everything about it that makes it more special than the other trees.

She started doing the same thing with some buildings they could see in the distance. Dacus picked one in particular.

Suddenly, a halo of white lights began to glow on the building's roof. Dacus smiled. 'I made it light up.'

I made it light up.

That's what we're doing here. We're choosing to pay attention to things and we're noticing what makes them special. We're increasing the sum total of specialness in the world.

(Alert: if we're not careful, one day we'll make everything special. And then nothing will be special any more. So let's keep an eye on that, people. It's like they say in *The Incredibles*: 'When everyone's super, no one will be'.)

Next time you have a spare five minutes, on a bus, in a waiting room, in a meeting, pay special attention to one particular thing out of several.

A tree. A pen. A ceiling tile.

Notice how it's the same as all the others and how it's different. Try and make it light up.

Jenny Owen founded the global insights agency Ruby Pseudo. She travels the world understanding what makes people tick. She's a savant at this kind of noticing. I asked her what she pays special attention to:

I suppose I notice patterns a lot, and the little discrepancies that do or don't make sense. I also tend to notice the subtleties in people's language and actions.

I people-watch a lot. I like to think I can 'read' people, without wanting to sound like a twit, but I've been talking to humans for nearly 45 years and studying them somewhat for over 20, so I think it's okay to say that. My partner tells me I'd be a good witness because I notice and read things quickly. Sometimes he tests me on a car reg we saw on a film or what colour someone's top was…

We've all heard about being properly present and the psychological benefits of being 'mindful'. Professor Ellen Langer was once interviewed about it by the *Harvard Business Review*:

'Mindfulness is the process of actively noticing new things. When you do that, it puts you in the present. It makes you more sensitive to context and perspective. It's the essence of engagement. And it's energy-begetting, not energy-consuming.'

And that's it. Noticing. It sounds incredibly banal, doesn't it? But it's literally and figuratively enlivening. Remind yourself to do it and the world lights up.

 DO 1

Focus on something in the room you're in. Just for a minute. Notice the patterns and the lack of patterns.

Made you look

I use an app called 1 Second Everyday to take, well, a second of video every day. Dailyish. Most days since January 2015.

The app makes it dead easy. I normally make them into monthly videos and bung them on my Vimeo account, where no one watches them. Occasionally, I'll go back and look at an old one and be reminded of a holiday we went on or an old café I used to love.

It forces you to keep an eye out for the visually interesting bits of your day. It dials up your attention.

(Ironically, most days are pretty much like all the others, so you end up with street scenes and cups of coffee and lift doors closing. And eventually that'll be the stuff the future finds fascinating. Whenever we watch a documentary featuring recovered footage from some famous historical event, the bits that stick out are the glimpses into everyday reality. Look at all the hats! Look at that street sign! How packed are the buses?!)

● **DO 2**
Do something visual every day for 30 days.

Remember it now

A little while ago a notebook brand called 'Field Notes' became all the rage with designers and digital people.

On the covers they said: 'I'm not writing it down to remember it later, I'm writing it down to remember it now'.

That's the essence of all this. I write in a notebook every day. But I almost never go back and look at what I wrote. Writing in a notebook is about transferring things from the world to your brain, not to your notebook.

Your notebook is a lens for looking at the world, not a box to keep it in.

Designer and futurist Anab Jain uses photos in a similar way:

[I take] lots and lots of photos. I have no idea how I'm going to archive them or organise them. But a lot of the time I'm taking photographs not to save and archive them in any specific way, but as a way of remembering and acknowledging the noticing.

 DO 3

Get yourself a little notebook. Write in it dailyish for a week. Or take a photo.

On the other hand, Denise says:

I love the idea of flipping back through my notebook, but it's just not what I do. My handwriting is terrible. I like scrubbing things out and redoing them. I can do that easier on screen than off. So even though I love special stationery, paper and pens, I write all my notes on my phone.

If I've noticed something interesting, I'll do one of two things:

1. *Write a couple of words about it, for example, 'Tiny dog, manic legs'.*

2. *Let it rattle around in my head a bit and write something a bit longer later, for example, 'Tiny, spindly dog, legs moving faster than the second-hand spring in a pocketwatch. Cyclical, rhythmical — but at first glance, absolutely manic.'*

I've chosen to write up the things I notice each week. And by keeping a digital note, I can open it on my phone, on the way to the office, or on my laptop, when I get to the office. That way, everything is kept in the order it happened. That's just what works for me.

You can read the magnificent results of Denise's phone-based note-taking at *walknotes.com*.

 DO 4

Create a 'noticings' file on your phone.
Put it on the Home screen.

Your way or the highway

And, of course, it doesn't have to be literally writing things down. Not everyone likes writing or can do it.

Loads of people have started using voice notes instead. That works. Or do a little sketch.

The key is to actively record something you've noticed. To consciously intervene so it doesn't just pop like a soap bubble the minute your brain moves on.

And if you've always been a notebook person, it's good to try other ways of doing it every now and then. Maybe the perfect habit is just an experiment away.

● **DO 5**
Spend a week taking notes in a way you've never done before.

Challenge Ant

Ant Harris is a communications strategist and generally interesting person. He's developed a habit of creating challenges for himself every year. I asked him to explain.

I'd come across a particularly life-affirming Venn diagram (yes, they do exist). Looking back now, I realise it's a little trite. But at the time, a year into my first ever 9-to-5 job, it struck a chord. I remember drawing it out (printer ink was too expensive) and sticking it to my wall. A constant reminder to myself that I didn't want to settle into the day-in, day-out rhythm of a life lived comfortably.

A few days later it was my 22nd birthday, and I decided to do something about it. There were two things I was certain of: first, I'm socially awkward enough that I won't leave my comfort zone unless I'm compelled to. And second, I'm a completist and hate an unfinished list.

I decided to see 22 gigs, all whilst I was 22. I posted 22 blank bullet points on my blog, and then set about filling them in. For my 23rd birthday, I decided to eat 23 foods I'd never tried — jellied eels, insects, braised squirrel, frogs' legs (and some less disgusting untried foods, too). And the year after that, 24 museums. Over the years, I've supped soups, wandered markets, shaken cocktails, walked cemeteries, even run with flaming barrels. Anything to force me out of routine, and keep my eyes open.

I'm now in my thirties, and faced with the grim reality that it's a lot harder now. Obviously. That's built in. The older I get, the more there is to do. But with every year, it also gets more necessary too. My comfort zone looks increasingly comfy. But I'm not ready to settle into it yet.

He's documented it all online at *antharris.co/challenges*. Sometimes with extensive blogposts and photos, sometimes not.

I go to my studio every day. Some days work comes easily. Other days nothing happens. Yet on the good days the inspiration is only an accumulation of all the other days, the non-productive ones.

Beverly Pepper

Compound interest for creativity

All of these little acts of attention are good in themselves but the real magic is in the repetition.

A tiny creative act, repeated, gets powerful, quickly.

Look at a tree. Take a photo. Could be a good photo. Might not be. It's just a tree. Take a photo the next day. It'll be different. Different light. Different weather. Different mood. Now you're not just noticing the tree, you're noticing the differences.

Do that for a week and you start to see more. Do it over a year, and you see the seasons. Do it for ten years and you'll see climate change.

Repetition over time gives us access to new visions. Things we couldn't see before.

James Bridle is a writer and artist once described as a 'sifter, collator and hacker of increasingly opaque technologies'. He experiments with this kind of thing a lot.

I was trying to understand plants for a long time, to get to know them, and one way people show how lively and interesting plants are is to use time-lapse photography.

At ten or twenty times the speed, it's easy to see how much plants actually move, how much individuality and personality they have, which isn't apparent at human timescales of perception. So I decided to make some time-lapses myself, and what I realised was that while the resulting little movies were nice, just like all those other ones on the internet and David Attenborough shows, that wasn't the point of what I did. I didn't speed up the plants: I slowed myself down to their speed.

That's what you actually have to do when you make time-lapses: you have to spend the actual time doing it, and you become aware of that time, you embody it, and you understand something different as a result. You actually get to know the plants, which was my intent, and is not achieved by just watching someone else do the thing.

Means, not ends, as Aldous Huxley always insisted; it's the doing that's interesting, it's the focus of that attention that makes everything else fluoresce.

This principle applies to all sorts of things.

It's not just photos. Do something once, it's great.
Do it twice, you add connections and time.

Keep doing it and those effects multiply. And then, if you do something adjacent, you get a whole heap of benefits.

You see the parallels, you get to compare and contrast. But, even more magically, if you're also doing something else entirely, suddenly you'll see that there are unexpected and unpredictable contrasts and comparisons.

But, *more importantly*, you do something to yourself. As James says, it's the doing that's important, not the output. It's where you put your attention.

 DO 6
Pick somewhere you go regularly. Find something you see all the time. Take a picture every time you pass by. Start to notice the changes. Do it 12 times.

Observing trifles

Arthur Davies is an actor. A lot of acting is about noticing — paying attention to the world of your character. I asked him about his favourite actorly noticing tricks.

Being Sherlock

Sherlock Holmes is famously good at noticing things. 'My method is founded on the observation of trifles.'

He glances at someone and can immediately tell that they're an impoverished accountant from Tewkesbury with a methadone habit. Or something.

He notices every tiny detail and builds up a story.

And no one can really do that. Sherlock is fictional (spoilers!). But you can pay that sort of attention and apply that sort of imagination. It's a fantastic way to actively attend to new people you meet. What do you notice about them? And what might that mean?

Maybe Michelle Obama is a secret Holmes. Her advice for meeting someone new is, 'Don't look around, don't look beyond them. Look them in the eye, take in the story.'

Being Smiley

In John Le Carré's Tinker Tailor Soldier Spy *the former spy George Smiley plays little noticing games to try and keep his brain from 'the atrophy of retirement'. He learns the names of the shops on his bus route to the British Museum. He counts how many stairs there are on each flight in his house and remembers which way each of his doors opens. Of course, he's not as retired as you might suspect and these little bits of tradecraft come in handy.*

Playing these little games yourself is a way to nudge yourself into noticing.

DO 7

Pick a favourite fictional character and try noticing the world through their eyes. Do it for an hour.

Your feet become ears

My favourite noticing guide is a book by Alexandra Horowitz called *On Looking*. She goes on a series of walks with various different professionals who point out the things that only they notice.

One of them is a sound designer who shows her how the sound of a city changes in the rain.

'It's dry now, but did you hear the sound of the tyres earlier?' I had not. 'Tyres actually stick to the pavement more because of the water when it rains,' he said. 'You can actually hear the sound of rubber on water; it's different than rubber on pavement.'

I love that so much, so I had to find a sound expert to talk to about noticing. And then I heard a podcast which included monthly soundscapes recorded by sound artist Alice Boyd.

I asked her to tell me a little about her work and how she pays attention to sound.

Over the last five years, I've worked as a composer and sound artist. It has been a meandering journey through different industries: music, theatre, podcasting and more.

But what has always been at the heart of my practice is my focus on the natural world and our place within it.

It wasn't until the first lockdown that I truly turned my focus towards listening. As the hum of cars and planes subsided and the chorus of birds and wildlife seemed louder than any spring before, many of us noticed this sonic silver lining of the pandemic.

It's rare that we take the time to sit and listen. However, if you can spare five minutes to close your eyes and notice the sounds around you (even the jarring ones), you may learn something new about the space you're in.

One of Alice's inspirations is the sound artist Pauline Oliveros. One of her musical scores reads simply this:

Take a walk at night. Walk so silently that the bottoms of your feet become ears.

 DO 8

Next time it rains, pop outside and notice how things sound different.

Don't just do something, stand there

Here's Denise again.

Most weekdays, whether I feel like it or not, I go for a walk before work. It's a habit that started during the pandemic. What I wanted to do was run, but I had issues with my back, so I made myself go for a walk instead: across the park; down the road; through the woods.

The mud arrived in the winter and at the same time, my walking boots fell apart. So in the weeks before I got new ones I forced myself to trudge around the streets instead. I resented it, but I needed the exercise.

I always walk on my own. So, to keep me going, I started looking for the one remarkable thing that I could take home with me, the one thing that was interesting enough to tell someone about later. It wasn't always easy, but there was usually something. Occasionally there was more than one thing, in which case, I forced myself to choose.

In my mock-Tudor neighbourhood, there are six art deco 'suntrap' houses. They're white, boxy, flat-roofed and completely different to every other house for miles.

The people who live in one pair of semi-detached mock-Tudor houses like each other so much, they've removed the divider in their front gardens. Instead, they share and maintain a beautiful, semi-circular rockery.

There's a house with a pine tree in the garden so huge that it blocks out the light for everyone inside. It also blocks their view of the most incredible roses in the garden. Squeezed in the space between the tree's thick branches and a bounding wall, you can only see the roses from the pavement. A wonderful sight for passers by, but rarely for the people who own them.

The writer Ronald Blythe wrote a long-running weekly column in the Church Times, called 'Word from Wormingford'. It's a telling of the comings and goings of life in a rural parish, the community that lives there and the changing of the seasons.

'Each morning,' he wrote, 'at about six, tea in hand, I sit for an hour looking out of the window, regular as clockwork.' He explains that, 'Windows have a way of limiting what one sees and, at the same time, intensifying the vision.'

If you're feeling pressure to notice the most incredible, remarkable things, don't. Sometimes the trick is just to look more closely at what's around you. Look for the things that are hiding in plain sight; try and find the magic.

Artists are good at it. Comedians are good at it. The best writers do it. Virginia Woolf, lying in bed while recovering from illness, wrote about the sky she could see through her window. In being forced to narrow her view, she really starts to see, and finds 'the sky is discovered to be something so different... that really it is a little shocking'. She describes the shapes, the movement, the colours and shadows.

'Ought not some one to write to The Times? *Use should
be made of it. One should not let this gigantic cinema play
perpetually to an empty house.'*

'This gigantic cinema'. How wonderful.

DO 9

**What's the best window with a view you can
spend 10 minutes in front of this month?
Have a gigantic cinema trip.**

Capitalist ruins

**Anab Jain is a co-founder and director of Superflux —
a boundary-defying, award-winning design and
experiential futures company. As you might expect,
Anab has a particular and fascinating way of paying
attention to the world.**

*I think what I tend to notice a lot are the conceptual
connections between things and ideas that may otherwise
go unnoticed. Whether it's a big news story or a faint signal,
I tend to see connections between that and something else
— an event, or an idea or a happening that is seemingly
unrelated. I'm trying to draw threads between, for instance,
ecology and economics, between art and finance — and
more, in an attempt to perhaps challenge the grand
narratives that have become the status quo, challenge what
we accept as 'normal', by noticing edge practices or practices
that may otherwise have fallen off the main narrative.*

*The other kind of stuff I notice is what we call nature.
I'm very interested in tiny, small things around me. So oddly
enough, I spend a lot of time looking down, especially
when I'm walking. I'm trained as a documentary filmmaker
and so I do a lot of quick photography on my phone.
I'm always trying to go on walks and end up taking*

hundreds of photographs of extreme close-ups of moss and spiderwebs, and dewdrops and textures of rocks and colours of autumn leaves, and lots of different types of mushrooms and so on. I'm really interested in the beauty of very, very little and tiny things in nature and around us.

Sometimes it's the small things that inform the big things. I am reminded of what Ursula Le Guin wrote, on reviewing Anna Tsing's book, The Mushroom at the End of the World: *'Scientists and artists know that the way to handle an immense topic is often through close attention to a small aspect of it, revealing the whole through the part. In the shape of a finch's beak we can see all of evolution.'*

The photographer Russell Duncan collects visual notes in a similar way. Often of the dozens (perhaps hundreds) of little objects he's kept to photograph, things that just feel like they have something interesting to say.

I often see the potential for something to end up in a photograph. Could be as a main subject, in a supporting role or as a background. Recently, for example, I broke a lovely handmade glass vase. It shattered into thousands of tiny bits but left three larger pieces, quite beautiful in their own way. I shot the shard of glass with daylight, trying three or four different colours and textures (see page 16). It took ten minutes at most. It serves as both a visual note and a bit of a prompt to take further pictures along similar lines.

 DO 10

Collect a visual note every day this week. Something without an explicit logical meaning, it just seems like you should shoot it.

Clear the decks

Clem has one more thing to say before this part ends...

She writes:

It's easy to put all of this kind of thing off.

There are loads of things — both serious and small — that we end up doing first. This is more true for some people than others. People with caring responsibilities. People working two jobs. Lots of women. Sometimes, that is just what's required, and that's okay.

But we can't ignore the fact that we can create the conditions that make the magic more possible. One needs a room of one's own.

This is not an unusual idea in many other walks of life: we train for a marathon, we grease a baking tin, we pebble ice before sliding curling stones across it.

In How to Have a Good Day, *economist Caroline Webb advises us not to waste our 'working memory' — the memory we use to think things through, connect things and plan. Too often, we cram our working memory with low-level brain tasks, like remembering to buy milk. She tells us:*

'Never waste your brain's precious working memory by trying to hold your tasks or ideas in your head. Use your intelligence for getting things done, rather than trying to remember what you need to do.'

The simplest way to do this is to write things down. Get that stuff out of your head. Dump the crap. This creates more room for the big thoughts. I write things in a notebook kept by the bed specifically for this purpose, often in the middle of the night.

Similarly, space and separation from what you're working on can be helpful. As psychologist and writer Maria Konnikova puts it in her book Mastermind: How to Think Like Sherlock Holmes, *'One of the most important ways to facilitate imaginative thinking is through distance.'*

Her theory is that Sherlock solves crimes where Watson does not because he is good at walking away from the mysteries he is trying to solve.

You're allowed to have a tea break. In fact, you should have a tea break.

And better yet, take that tea outside. Go for a walk. Forget about it. Call your mum.

When you go back to whatever you were working on, you'll make it better.

 DO 11
Have a break. Have a KitKat.

PART 2

COLLECTING

Research is formalised curiosity. It is poking and prying with a purpose.

Zora Neale Hurston

Now you've got to turn all these things you've noticed into something you can use. A compost of thoughts and connections.

Noticing is good. Storing and remembering what you've noticed is great. It turns your noticing into research. You'll remember more of what you've noticed. You'll collide ideas together, which will multiply the value of everything. And you'll learn something about yourself, your own passions and interests.

The slow hunch and the spark file

The writer Steven Johnson has two very helpful big notions about how ideas happen and how to collect them.

The slow hunch

This is his challenge to the popular wisdom that great breakthroughs come from sudden moments of revelation: Archimedes in his bath or Newton under his apple tree.

Johnson says that that's not really how great ideas come into the world. He suggests that it's actually a slower and bumpier road. Most of the time, people mull on these things for years. Hunches, vague thoughts, bundles of possibilities, without crystallised problem statements or obvious solutions.

Yes, sometimes the final thought will pop up as you stand in a shower or sit under an apple tree. But interesting ideas normally come from the slow accumulation of related thoughts, questions and ponderings.

Johnson cites Tim Berners Lee's long, slow progress on the invention of the World Wide Web. This took years, with TBL dipping in and out, abandoning it, working on something else, coming back to it, etc.

Or Darwin's slow poking at natural selection. Darwin believed it came to him in a sudden flash but, looking at his journals, historians have realised that he had all the components for it gathered and understood for years before that moment.

If you want to cultivate ideas, you need to let them stew. Your stew will be tastier if you let your attention drift into other areas of study, adjacent worlds where there might be concepts that will help you.

You need to be prepared to think long and wide. And you'll need some tools and practices to help you do that.

The spark file

Johnson's other idea is simple but powerful.

It's just a text document where he writes down all the thoughts, ideas, possibilities and fragments of language that occur to him.

Just one after the other, as they come up, in a long chronological list. Simple, right?

The genius bit is that he has the discipline to go back and read it every six months or so. And when he re-reads it he'll often be reminded of some old idea that suddenly has new relevance, or that suddenly fits with something else.

It's a scrapbook for ideas, but the regular review keeps it fresh in his head.

He's outsourced the hard part — remembering all the detail — but he keeps the potentially important stuff fresh in his working memory.

I talked to the comic-book artist Ramsey Hassan about this stuff. He does something similar:

I used to print out articles and put them in box files but it got too crazy so now I copy and paste articles into a huge Word doc or screenshot stuff. Sometimes it's immediately useful and sometimes I store it away and six months or three years later another idea would spark with it and I go back to look up the detailed idea because I only remember the broad strokes.

So does the writer and artist James Bridle:

I keep these incredibly long Word documents on the go, just copying and pasting little snippets into them, having them open to type into while on the phone to people, links, URLs, etc. They usually start focused on a particular subject, and then wander all over the place — the same goes for a bunch of Tumblr blogs I post to. These documents become projects if they get long enough. They might turn into an artwork or a collaboration.

Whole books have started this way: my last book was all based around a fifty-page Word doc I'd kept running for about two years. The document wasn't the book, not even a draft of it, but it contained enough things that I could start writing something solid, and return back to if I ran out of steam.

 DO 12

Start a spark file. Make some sort of note or calendar invite to look at it again in six months.

The principle of limited sloppiness

Virginia Woolf described her ideal diary:

I should like it to resemble some deep old desk or capacious hold-all, in which one flings a mass of odds and ends without looking them through. I should like to come back, after a year or two, and find that the collection had sorted itself and refined itself and coalesced, as such deposits so mysteriously do.

You're noting stuff down, taking photos, keeping your eyes open and your ears pricked. What do you do with it all?

Simple. Fling your mass of odds and ends into a capacious hold-all. Things do mysteriously sort and refine themselves. Banging things together makes them more interesting.

You can do this in an efficient and organised manner. You can use coloured folders and identically sized boxes. If that's the sort of person you are, then fabulous.

But don't worry about it if you're not.

In fact, there's probably some advantage in keeping it all messy.

Max Delbrück was a Nobel laureate who studied physics and biology. He obviously believed that scientists should be careful and rigorous in their work. But he thought that a bit of looseness was helpful too, as it allowed room for the unexpected and accidental. He called this the Principle of Limited Sloppiness.

Similarly there's lots of evidence that although the frenzied multitasking of everyday life is probably a bad thing, having a few different longer-term projects happening at once is good for creativity.

Ideas slip from one project to another and the cross-pollination makes everything richer and punchier.

And, importantly, most ideas come to people when they're not trying to have them.

The cliché of the idea that comes in the shower is true. Working on different projects at the same time enhances this effect. And you can manifest this in the bagginess of your capacious hold-all.

 DO 13

Could you get yourself a capacious hold-all?
A Word doc will do. Or a shoe box.

Counting counts

There's a magic in the accumulation of things, or of data.

'Temperature blankets' or 'temperature scarves' are an accumulation of noticings. People who knit or crochet choose a set of colours and allocate a temperature range to each. Perhaps sunset yellow is 25–30 degrees, for example. Every day at a certain time they note the temperature and knit or crochet a row in a colour that corresponds to the temperature. And at the end of the year they have a beautiful blanket or scarf charting the changing of the seasons.

You can chart other things too. The time the sun comes up, or sets. How much rain falls each month. How often the train is late. It takes the pressure off noticing something momentous every day.

You can choose what you do with that information. Make a piece of art, adjust your alarm clock, start a campaign for better rail services.

The designer Stef Posavec is a genius at this kind of data collection and creativity. She writes extraordinary books that use data to captivate and explain. I asked her what she does and how she does it.

I like to say that the main material I create and communicate with is data, often personal data gathered by hand. I see the world with the eyes of a 'data collector'. We are surrounded by so many invisible, interesting data points and patterns just waiting to be collected!

Data collection is inherently creative. Depending on the data you choose to collect from the world, you can begin to see the world from a different perspective. Being a data collector means observing the world with curiosity.

Lately I have asked myself:

On my street/housing estate of about 106 houses:

— I wonder how many different cats live here?
  (there are quite a few)

— I wonder how many different houses each of these cats like to visit? (they pop into multiple houses asking for food)

— I wonder how many houses own a car?

In regards to my parenting:

— I wonder how many times every single meal I end up asking my energetic, excited five-year-old to sit back down in her seat?

— How many times am I actually asking her to do something before she will learn to do it without me asking? 500? 1,000 times? More?

Then I:

— *visualise the data as part of an artwork*

— *use it to inform the development of data-driven art commissions*

— *use it to reflect on a part of my life I want to look at more closely*

— *treasure the data as a diary/souvenir/memento of a moment in time*

 DO 14

Count something. Every day for a month. Visualise it.

Focus on what stirs you up inside, what is beautiful and true.

Ali Montag

Gotta catch 'em all

Clearly, you should collect whatever you fancy. And some things are obvious: images, quotes, facts.

But there are non-obvious things that will come in handy one day.

Analogies, metaphors, ideas, models, assumptions, habits, patterns, vibes, objects that express ideas, images that evoke occasions, things you don't understand yet but that you feel will mean something one day.

Collect those too.

The soft openness
of a scrapbook

**Physical scrapbooks work by being tools for what
the psychologist Ellen Langer calls 'soft openness':**

*What you want is a soft openness — to be attentive to the
things you're doing but not single-minded, because then
you're missing other opportunities.*

Navaz Batliwalla is an author, stylist and fashion blogger.
She has scrapbooks:

*I'm like a scrapbook myself. I'm very hybridy. Taking things
from different places and then hacking them together in
whatever context.*

*I love collage and when I went to college I actually wanted
to be an illustrator. The course was called fashion
promotion, illustration and photography. The course
was like a collage itself.*

*One of my good friends was into collage and he made these
beautiful scrapbooks. And I got this really amazing one with
different coloured papers. It was massive and quite expensive
so I just keep stuffing and stuffing and stuffing. So now I've
got to the point where all my scrapbooks are completely
overstuffed and now I just use boxes and carrier bags.*

Bags full of scraps. I tend to revisit them all the time. And I tend to play with the scraps rather than actually putting them in the scrapbook. Once you commit to the scrapbook, it feels finished. So you are torn. How do I use this? Do I commit it to this or to something else?

It's so relaxing and even in the process of putting scraps together, your mind wanders. Maybe I do it every six months and all the things that happened during that time mean you're looking at the scraps in a different way. It has a different meaning. Maybe a scrap then goes with something else.

And if I'm starting a big project, like a book, you can just get the scraps out and start going through them, pulling things out and making a new pile and a new way of thinking.

It's amazing because although I know my scrapbooks and my boxes quite well now, there are always things that I've forgotten about. Something that I kept, not knowing what it would be for.

 DO 15

If you've already got a scrapbook, go and have a leaf through. If you haven't, maybe it's time.

Hey there,
moody chops

A scrapbook is a collection. A mood board is a decision.

It's specific, delineated and precise. It's there to put a hard border around something vague and floaty: a mood, a vibe, a feeling.

That's what makes a mood board so useful. But tricky to do well.

Navaz told me about the book she wrote based on a mood board:

It started with a Pinterest board that was all this particular style, which I call 'gentle woman style', which came from a few places. The name came from the The Gentlewoman *magazine, which came out about 10 years ago. It was very classic, masculine/feminine, quite a particular aesthetic.*

And then when I was asked if I was interested in publishing a book, I was able to use that to explain it to the publishers and to find these very specific women, not just how they dress, but their attitudes and approach.

Notice the words in there: 'specific', 'particular'.

The film director Mira Nair taught a masterclass about making movies and emphasised the importance of a lookbook (essentially the same thing as a mood board). She describes it as 'a manifesto of visual references'.

It's important to have a point of view about the aesthetic and of the design of the story.

For her film *Monsoon Wedding*, Nair rejected the clichés Hollywood loves to use for India and selected colours that are very specifically Indian: indigo, ochre and burgundy. Her lookbook communicated that to everyone involved in the film so that, for instance, when extras turned up for a scene, they knew what colours they should be wearing.

That's the sign of a useful mood board. It helps with decisions. For yourself or your collaborators. You should be able to look at it and rule stuff in or out.

— **Start wide:** Get too much stuff. Anything that might fit.

— **Take your time:** Keep coming back to it. See it with fresh eyes. Prune. Get rid of anything that doesn't clarify.

— **Look beyond the Pantone:** A colour's never just a colour. A pink building says something different to a pink cardigan.

 DO 16
**Create the mood board for the short film
you're going to make someday.**

Find out who you are and do it on purpose.

Dolly Parton

Make a virtue of your peculiarities

In her novel *The Dispossessed*, Ursula Le Guin has one of her characters say this: 'There's a point, around the age of twenty, when you have to choose whether to be like everybody else the rest of your life, or to make a virtue of your peculiarities.'

This is where interestingness comes to life. When you use your personal preferences, interests and delights to shape your noticing and collecting. There are, of course, a ton of different ways to do this…

Jump-start with a mind map

Jeffre Jackson is the thinker and strategist who got me started on 'interestingness' in the first place. His approach to thinking about what interests him, and thinking with it, is typically, brilliantly peculiar.

I think that interestingness is based on pattern recognition and that the more connections you see, the more interesting the world becomes. So, I keep a chart that reminds me of some of the things that I've been interested in for a long time.

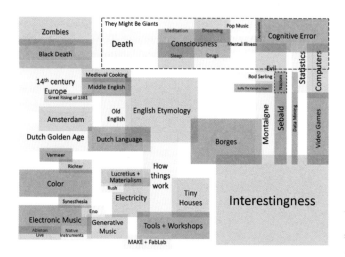

© Jeffre Jackson

*I can jump-start my interestingness engine just by imagining
possible connections between any of these topics.
(E.g. the band Rush × electronic music: Given Rush's love of
complexity, what does it mean that they insisted on playing
everything themselves, even when they acknowledged that
it was a huge pain in the ass to learn and play many of
their own songs? Many of their songs are celebrations
of technology and just as many are about the dangers
of technology. What effect might this double-sided
attitude have on their teenage nerd fanbase? If Rush had
programmed more of their music, would they still be called
'progressive rock'?)*

 DO 17
Make a mind map like Jeffre's. Revisit it.

Dredge the swampy canal

The photographer Jim Marsden has an omnivorous appetite for influences and ideas, most of which, at first blush, have nothing much to do with photography.

He teaches photography and gives sets of gorgeous inspiration cards to his students, illustrated by printmaker Hannah Cousins. One of them sums up this approach. It's called Fill Your Library.

FILL YOUR LIBRARY.

Without libraries what have we?
We have no past and no future.

– Ray Bradbury

In your mind is a library, and it is unique.

It is different from every one of the other seven and a half billion human beings on this planet.

From this unique library, you will pull inspiration to make your work, and it's your responsibility to look after it and keep it replenished.

So, read widely from poetry to fiction to biography.

Listen to music, try different types and styles (it's never been easier)

Be aware of your experiences in life, both the good and the bad (you need both).

Fill your library every day, because this is the fuel for your work.

FILL YOUR LIBRARY.

© 2017 Jim Marsden

Jim says:

Watch a film, read a book, have a conversation. Nothing is wasted! Don't squeeze it in, don't force it in ... leave your mind to it. Say to it: you decide what's important.

I start a project. Sit down and think about what could connect with it. Go back into the references — dredge the swampy canal — and see what connects ... When I take photos, I aim for zero thinking. Instead, I recognise or connect with references I've built up over time and SNAP! Everybody should fill the library they have inside ... Only you have the body of references you have.

The comic-book artist Ramsey Hassan is similarly wide-ranging. He told me:

I feel that it's all about what connects with you. I saw a documentary on TV about transhumanism that not only blew my mind but sparked an idea that became a short story. The next day I was perusing the shelves of a bookstore and overheard a couple of the booksellers there discussing that same documentary — essentially making fun of these crackpot tech guys trying to create extra senses. In the same way a piece of art might resonate — I feel it's the same for information too. Creative-minded people's brains are hungry for the next spark and anything remotely interesting will trigger it.

 DO 18
Seek out influences and inspiration that are far away from what you're working on.

Read around

Another way to 'go at' an interest is to come at it from different angles. Sneak up on it. See what someone else has to say.

This happened to Clem when she read Gabriel García Márquez's novel about Simón Bolívar, the man who liberated six South American countries from Spanish colonial rule. Like lots of books that capture the imagination, she read it by accident.

I became hooked on the story of this small, capable, bonkers man who had achieved so much but was so little known outside of the continent he came from. From the novel, I went to the biography (Marie Arana's, it's very good). Then I went to 4 Duke Street in Marylebone, the house Bolívar stayed in during his trip to London in 1810. I read some obscure blog posts about Daniel O'Leary, his Irish aide-de-camp, a native of Cork. I tried the Netflix series about him (don't bother). There is no set destination to all this investigation, I'm just enjoying the ride.

Just like a country is more enjoyable to visit when you've read a novel set there (if you haven't tried this trick, do it), any topic is more interesting if you've explored it from the edges.

Plus, you'll find out things that relate to other bits stored in the filing cabinet of your brain. And it's these connections that make your 'library' unique. For example, Bolívar's story is, to my mind, connected to Michelle Obama, the relationship between topography and democracy, and my sister-in-law's hairdresser!

James Bridle is an inveterate read-arounder too:

Something seems interesting enough to make a mark about it, but you also leave the door open: you don't see that thing in isolation, you start to notice other things that are like it in some way. Or, crucially, you start to notice a territory that is defined by these apparently disparate but actually related things, some aspect which links them, and by linking them you bring a bunch of other things into view, things which lie on some kind of spectrum around or between the first things: this is the territory.

This isn't brain work, it's heart work, at least initially, and the heart has its own senses and ways of thinking about things, and you can trust it just to do its thing for a while.

 DO 19

Circle the thing you're working on at the moment. Google it. Look up the etymology. See if there's some fiction about it. Go around.

↑shriked by *
Hen Harrier (r.t.)
1/11 <u>Parkgate</u>
4pm Hen Harrier ♂ ♂ *↑
Marsh Harrier, 1, 1.
Bittern, stretching,
Showing head and
neck (then flew away
looking into the sun
Barn Owl* prolonged
View over marsh
179 Grey Heron

2/12 West Kirby M.L.

Cheshire first

11/12 Ligwy Bay, Anglesey
Arr 11.10am Royal Tern fecum
1pm. Very distant flying in b
Razorbill 1.
Shag 1, 1.
Great Northern Dive

STATS & FACTS
Only previous British
record: South Stack,
Anglesey, 4-5 October 2001
Only previous Irish record:
Cape Clear, Co Cork, 4
November 1986
Previous Western
Palearctic records: 9
Mega rating: ★★★★★

Anglesey bird
was very elusive

TOP 20   2019/20
8/4 Iceland Gull 2nd W   Sefton Park
19/4 Grasshopper Warbler   Leasowe
24/4 Dotterel (3) ♂♂,♀ ↑   Great Orme
28/4 Spanish Wagtail ♂   Leasowe
17/5 Stilt Sandpiper 6th   Lunt.
24/5 White-winged Tern   BMW 3rd
31/5 Stone Curlew, ad/2CH   Mins mere
1/6 Turtle Dove   Titchwell
15/6 Savi's Warbler 8th   Maltrach
      Manx Shearwater 20+   Cemlyn
10" Red-backed Shrike ♂   Great Or
17/6 Red-backed Shrike ♂   BMW
19/6 Sandwich Tern (4)
3/7 Gull-billed Tern, ad 5th   Thurst
8/8 Little Bustard ♂ 2nd   Mick
21/9 American Golden Plover (2)
9/10 Kentish Plover W.P. 5th
27/12 Siberian Stonechat 1st W
19/1 Snow Bunting (2) Rhy
12/2 Red-breasted Merganser
24/2 Long-billed Dowitche

Dive deep

Not everyone is this kind of wide-ranging generalist. Some people prefer to focus. They have a real passion for a particular thing. This works too.

As the early environmentalist John Muir once wrote, 'When we try to pick out anything by itself, we find it hitched to everything else in the universe.'

As long as we're paying attention it's a stairway to interesting.

Here's an example, Anne's dad, my father-in-law:

Ron, my dad, has been birdwatching for more years than anyone can remember. At 90, rumour has it, he is the oldest birdwatcher in Cheshire. For most of those years, birdwatching was just 'Dad's thing', something he shared only tangentially with the rest of us. He'd get up early, drive across the country with people called Roger and John. He'd stand in a field/wood/outside someone's garden to see 'a lifer' or a first for the year, then drive back late at night, with telescope, binoculars and an empty flask.

Our family holidays were arranged with one eye on 'what might be around'. Red-legged partridges in windy Norfolk, ptarmigans in the chilly, off-season Cairngorms. A few times a year, he was picked up at 4am by Roger or John, on their way to somewhere more exotic. The Camargue, Iceland, Texas. In the 1970s and 80s these were not everyday places.

He brought my sister and me vases decorated with lava from Iceland and little pottery Dutch girls after staying with the elegant birdwatchers from Holland. He had other hobbies over the years — standing on the Kop at Liverpool, collecting stamps, betting on the horses. The last of these he stopped overnight, maybe before I was born, the first he now does in spirit, from his armchair. All were done with quiet, intelligent dedication.

We, his family, were not invited in, but neither did we really ask.

But then I hit middle age. Along with hot flushes and worrying about pensions, I've started to notice birds. As I tramp around Derbyshire, or stand on a Cornish estuary, I've found myself looking up and noticing. I would text my dad (via my mum — my dad doesn't do technology, obvs), describing something I'd seen and asking for a view. At the tail-end of one summer, I found myself on the Yorkshire coast at the same time as an albatross. My dad, in his late eighties, had already made the cross-country trip to see it, so sent me directions via text. And with the help of other birdwatchers, I did see it. Far out to sea and little more than a dot, but I did see it.

And so a birder is born. My dad gave me a pair of binoculars he'd won in a competition, and showed me how to use them. In that first outing with him, I learned that not all ducks are born equal and that listening is more important than looking. But mostly I saw my dad in his other world, where his years of doing make him infinitely interesting.

I am still on page one of the birder's life, but here are some of the things Ron has shared with me. Noticing and collecting are the backbone of being a lifelong birder.

What do you notice?

The first thing birders will notice is birdsong. I probably know the birdsongs of most British birds, so I am listening for something different. When you start birdwatching, you need to spend time learning 20 common birds and their songs, and then another 20. You'll start to notice the different when you can spot the usual.

And then there are bird calls, which are different to songs, harder to identify. Is it a contact call or a danger call? But the type of call will be limited by the habitat, time of year, location. Those things will tell you how easy it is going to be to spot the bird. You can hear something like a Cetti's warbler but spend all day trying to spot it in the willows. Some people are better at calls and songs than others and it's great to be out with a birder who can recognise birds you can't.

Once you spot the bird, it's all about 'the jizz'. How does the bird move, fly and walk? Think about how a pied wagtail walks, it's unmistakable. Look at a bird's shape, its beak, its feet. With experience, you learn to scan these things, again looking for something different, unfamiliar. You must be patient. Despite what we see on TV, nature doesn't just appear to order. And in general, birders don't like cheats. Sometimes you come across someone playing a song on their phone to tempt a bird out, but it's viewed badly. You don't really want a bunch of birders tutting at you.

How do you collect what you have seen?

In a notebook. Well, several notebooks. Birdwatchers will keep lists, a lot of them. I have one for Burton Mere where I go most often. Some people have a garden list. We'll all have an annual list and country lists and, of course, a life list. (Currently, I am up to 503.) I record where I saw a bird and when, sometimes describing the circumstances.
I don't start a new book every year or have to use exactly the same make of book. I'll also include some pictures (I don't take photographs). These days, people use apps and phone lists, but most birdwatchers still have some kind of physical notebook. Technology has changed things but not fundamentally.

© Ron Shewring

🔵 DO 20
Pick something you love and go deep.* Keep lists.

*And don't be embarrassed about it. As the actor Katharine Hepburn said, 'If you always do what interests you, at least one person is pleased.'

Cross the streams

At the heart of all this collecting is a big simple, joyous technique.

The best ideas happen when you bang things together. It's what makes a slow hunch work, it's what a spark file's for, it's what makes a scrapbook or mood board useful. The juxtaposition of unexpected or unfamiliar elements. That's what you should be practising here.

In the 1910s and 20s the filmmaker Lev Kuleshov did a number of experiments with film montages. He juxtaposed images of a Russian actor, Ivan Mosjoukine, with, variously, footage of some soup, a woman in a coffin or a girl playing with a toy. These films were then shown to audiences and they were asked what emotions they thought the actor was portraying.

One of his fellow experimenters reported: *The result was terrific. The public raved about the acting of the artist. They pointed out the heavy pensiveness of his mood over the forgotten soup, were touched and moved by the deep sorrow with which he looked on the dead woman, and admired the light, happy smile with which he surveyed the girl at play.*

The trick was that it was always the same bit of footage of Mosjoukine. Only the film he was juxtaposed with changed. The audience were bringing their own emotions and expectations to bear. This is now known as the Kuleshov Effect and explains the success of many very blank-looking Hollywood actors.

Juxtaposition works. So mix things up.

Pursue more than one interest. Stick things that look different next to each other. Move things around. Make something a fixed point and move other ideas/objects/pictures around it to see what happens. Make your interests messy. This is how slow hunches happen. It's also a really good creative shortcut.

The human brain is so desperate to find meaning in things that it will make a story out of any two random things put together. Images, words, sounds … anything. And that meaning can be more interesting than anything you were actually planning. Put music over an image and both get more interesting. Put a word next to another word and they both say something new.

This urge to juxtapose is critical to getting all these creative elements into your work. Stick the things you've collected into your presentations. You'll find that suddenly, somehow you're making a bigger, better point. Throw the writers you love or the notes you've taken into the writing you do for your job. It'll get more noticed and more effective.

Get comfortable with crossing the streams. It's where the best ideas come from.

In fact, when 'deep work' is becoming a religion, it's worth striking a heretical note: multitasking can be good. It might not help when you're trying to do something detailed and focused, but shallow work, skipping from one thing to the next — juxtaposing your activities — often produces the magic.

In her 'Science of Creativity' newsletter, Annie Murphy Paul wrote about a study in the journal *Organizational Behavior and Human Decision Processes* which demonstrates:

Task switching increases creativity. If you want to be creative, you should actually be switching tasks a lot more than you are already.

Forcing people to switch frequently between two different tasks increased their creativity in two ways:

1. *It improved their ability to generate multiple ideas, heading in diverse directions;*

2. *It improved their ability to identify the unique or best solution to the problem.*

Switching tasks helps reduce something called cognitive fixation, the tendency to get stuck in one particular approach to a problem. Turning to another task gets us out of this rut, seeing different possibilities.

This effect is so powerful that the authors of the study say:

People discount the creative efficacy of continual task switching, such that they overwhelmingly fail to select the condition that yields the best creative performance.

That's the thing to remember with your collection. It should be a mixed bag.

 DO 21

Next time you're writing a presentation, try something — paste random images onto every slide, whatever's on your desktop or on your phone. Just grab stuff.
Then make the presentation work with those images.
I bet it'll get more interesting.

PART 3

SHARING

Art does not come from thinking but from responding

Sister Corita Kent

If you've diligently followed all the suggestions so far then you'll be a little creative powder keg, ready to explode.

1. **You're good at finding things interesting**, at sticking with things that other people dismiss and looking beneath the surface. You can see what's distinctive or revealing about stuff that others find boring. You can light up a tree.

2. **You're used to capturing ideas.** Writing them down. Tearing them out of magazines. Grabbing them with your phone. Swapping them with friends.

3. **You have a capacious hold-all,** full of thoughts, notions, references, asides and treats.

4. **You have a sense of what your interests are,** or what sparks a light in you. What makes you peculiar.

Now you can start the real work. You can start making new stuff with it and sharing it with the world.

You have to transform what you've learned, make something new. Something interesting to share.

And this can be hard. If you're not used to doing 'creative' things, this is where imposter syndrome comes in.
Or embarrassment. Or fear of failure.

You have to assert something about yourself. Stand behind an idea. That can be daunting.

But that's why we did all the previous work — the noticing and collecting — because it means you're more than halfway there. You just need to nudge it over the line.

No point doing a dinosaur movie

The massive thing to remember here is that having an idea is not the important bit. Ideas become worthwhile and magic when you execute them.

Your idea might have been done a thousand times before, but you doing it, in your peculiar way, will inevitably make it personal and special.

One of the best idea-doers around is Rob Manuel, serial inventor of online wonders like b3ta and @fesshole. He talked to Denise about a Twitter conversation he'd had about ideas:

Someone replied saying how hard it is to come up with something new. But it doesn't matter about something having been done before, what matters is what you can bring to it by you being you. Imagine Spielberg going, 'No point doing a dinosaur movie, they've all been done.'

I write entirely
to find out
what I'm thinking,
what I'm looking at,
what I see and
what it means.

Joan Didion

Actually do the thing

James Bridle is a great example of someone who works this way. I asked him what advice he'd give to people who want to 'create'.

Actually do the thing, don't just read about it. If you're interested in how a thing works, build it. Even a shonky DIY version, or a paper model of it. Play with it at different scales.

One of my tricks is to draw stuff out on the ground and just sit with that: I've done it with drones (unmanned aerial vehicles), satellites, buildings and imaginary locations, either as chalk on the ground, or as what the Swiss call Baugespanne — ghost structures using poles and ropes or even balloons to visualise unbuilt things (this is a good metaphor for non-physical projects, like writing, too).

Make the thing that exists in your head real in some simple way; it will change it. Then learn how to do the next version: wood, plastic, code, whatever. You can learn to do it, and doing is an essential, non-negotiable component of understanding something.

One trick I use a lot, if I'm intimidated by the requirements of a project (as I often am, because most of the time I am doing something for the first time), is not to say, 'I am going to do this,' but to say, 'I am going to learn to do this,' because then I'm comfortable starting knowing nothing, and at the end I've still done the thing.

● **DO 22**
Build *Baugespanne*.

Writing on the internet

When I did the original 'How To Be Interesting' presentation, my number one piece of advice was 'Start a blog'.

That's still the advice. The easiest way to start sharing — your noticings, your collections, your ideas — and to make it into something of your own is to write stuff on the internet. And the easiest way to do that is to start a blog.

There are a ton of reasons to do it:

— It's an easy way to practise sharing in public

— It builds into an archive of your thoughts

— It can incorporate any medium you like

It's also a way to find your peeps and dial up your interesting. The blogger Henrik Karlsson put it well in a blog post entitled 'A blog post is a very long and complex search query to find fascinating people and make them route interesting stuff to your inbox'.

(I love it when the title tells you everything you need to know.)

He says that you should ignore all the usual advice about writing for a general audience. You should just be incredibly specific, precise and excited about exactly what interests you (in all its variety and apparent randomness) because the way that search engines and the social dynamics of the internet work mean that if there's anyone out there with similar interests, they will find you. They will be delighted to find another member of their tribe and they will start sending you stuff relating to whatever you've been blogging about.

Trust me, this happens.

So much of what I've learned about interestingness, creativity, ideas and getting things done has come through blogging about it and people who know more than me sending me stuff.

The important thing to remember is:

You are not wasting your time

Even after 20 years of blogging, of it clearly being a productive, creative, extraordinarily fecund means of communication, you will get people sniffily telling you you're wasting your time. 'You must have a lot of time on your hands,' they will tell you. It's especially likely to come from gate-keepers in traditional creative industries. They don't like the fact that we no longer need them.

Don't let this put you off. You're unlikely to spend more time on blogging than you would on any other hobby or form of professional development. And it'll be much more fun and rewarding.

The internet will tell you how to blog, you don't need me doing that.

But if you're worried about making that first mark, then you can work your way up to it.

— **You could start on LinkedIn.** It's easy to mock the everyone's-always-crushing-it vibe but it's a great place to venture out with some writing.

— **You could just do longer captions on Instagram.** Create some mini-essays and build from there.

— **You could use a service like Medium for a while.** It handles loads of the design choices for you. Don't forget, though, when you're posting on someone else's platform, you always risk it disappearing. You don't own any of it.

— **Or you could start a newsletter.** They seem all the rage these days. And, for some reason, people seem less sniffy about them. Perhaps because they appear more focused and commercial. But they don't have to be. Mine, for instance, actually is a waste of time.*

* buttondown.email/russell

DO 23
Start a blog, obvs.

Lists, diaries and weeknotes

If you're stuck for some ways to start, here are three formats you could try: lists, diaries and weeknotes.

52 things you won't believe about lists

You'll have noticed how popular lists are on the internet. And everywhere. They're not just fun to read, they're easy to write. A constraint and a format all rolled into one.

Tom Whitwell is a genius at lists. You might have seen his '52 Things I Learned In (This Year)'. He's been writing it since 2014.

I talked to Tom and tried to work out what some of his interestingness habits are and what he looks for and avoids for his 52 Things:

I suppose part of it is a strong thing about looking for something that you haven't seen before and you don't think other people have seen before. So there's a really basic thing of being allergic to something that feels like it's a press release. If they've sent it to everybody and everybody's just written [it] up and said, 'Here's the new thing,' then it's unlikely to be interesting.

Like today, I came across a company which has an enormous campus in Georgia in the US. They specialise in disaster preparedness and they have two city blocks of collapsed buildings to practise search and rescue. And I thought obviously, they must do. How else are you gonna train to do it? And as soon as you read that, you want to see a picture of it. And if you click on their website, the first thing's an enormous picture of basically a fallen-down city block.

And it feels like there's something kind of authentic about it. They're just cracking on with their business, which is helping people train for disaster preparedness. But by doing that, they've created something really extraordinary and unexpected. That's the quality I'm looking for.

One of the highlights of my blogging career was getting a Thing into one of Tom's lists of Things. And that's part of the joy of sharing on the internet. He can only do his lists because people share. And he boosts them and it all goes round again. It can be lovely.

 DO 24
Start a list. Capture a thing a week for 10 weeks.
Write a blog post about them all.

My granddad is keeping busy

One of the things I've learned from organising the Interesting conferences is the value of obliquity. People who just talk about themselves tend to be boring. People who let slip something about themselves while talking about something that excites them are invariably fascinating.

A similar thing goes for blogging. A great way to start is to share something small but personal. A hobby, something local. Or something from your family history.

Here's Anne again:

My granddad died in 1983. For the previous 20 years, Lee Edwards, my mum's dad, kept a diary, recording his day as a farm worker and then through his retirement. All the entries are in block capitals, often in pencil. As he gets older, and I think sicker, his writing becomes shakier, but he never misses a day. Over 20 years of a person's life in handy chunks — what a gift.

The first diaries are kept in May and Baker Ltd veterinary diaries, available free from his work. They are small, pocket-sized, mustard-coloured books, with four days to a double spread. Later, when he'd stopped working, he used hardbacked A5 diaries, sometimes from Boots. He made one book last four years by dividing each page into four sections. I think I remember the event of buying him a new diary.

Lee spent his whole life working outside, so the weather is a major character. 'Still cold and cloudy with rain nearly all morning. Dry after dinner but no sunshine. Went to get my toes done.' He lists the tasks of his day and later, when he retired, what was happening at the allotment. He tells us about the Wheatsheaf and we hear how Liverpool are doing. He is an old-school patriot and often sentimental.

'It's a New Year's Day yet again and I hope it will be a better one for my dear country than the last awful year with its riots and unemployment. I also hope it will be a good one for my beloved family.'

His entries are mundane, repetitive, sometimes mysterious (what does the occasional X mean?). He combines the everyday with news snapshots — 'N did the washing and ironing. I watered some seeds I put in the greenhouse. Gracie Fields was buried in Capri today' — and often leaves us hanging — 'Cut some wood up from the turkey pens. Went to the police about hole.' Like all of us, he is not straightforward. Occasionally there are moments which no longer sit well, but for a man who left school at 14, he read Shakespeare, Dickens and more — 'Good bath in the afternoon. No visitors came. Did some reading about Peter the Great of Russia. He was a remarkable man.'

Lee suffered from rheumatoid arthritis, so was in constant pain, but you would never know it. My mum once described him as a contented man, and reading these entries, you would have to agree. He didn't ask for much and genuinely lived a glass-half-full life. How many of us can say that? 'N rang the National Insurance people about my pension. They are sending me a Giro. Very civil of them.'

Lee's diaries sat on my shelf for years before I started to share the entries on a blog: mygranddadiskeepingbusy.com

Every day I post the matching entry, starting in 1962. It's nothing grand but people have said they find it enjoyable, peaceful even. Sometimes I post a photograph, either of him or someone else in my family. That's fun to do, like curating your own family. If an entry doesn't make sense, my mum, herself now in her late eighties, can often fill me in.

This daily blog post is a lovely way to spend a moment not just with someone who has gone but with a bit of my own life, my own history. It's made me think more about my own diary and what I keep and say. It's like me noticing again all the things he noticed years ago. I hope my granddad would be happy with that.

 DO 25
Is there something from your life, or your family's life, some little piece of mundane history, that you could share like this? Do 10 entries.

Weeknotes

If 'do blogging' is too big and vague as an instruction, here's a way to dip your toe in. Do weeknotes.

They're a good way to nudge yourself into paying attention — not just to the big things, but little things too.

Denise explains…

The idea of a public 'weeknote' came from digital teams who wanted to record their weekly progress: when work is happening quickly, it's often hard to see how far you've come or to understand how you've got there.

Writing weeknotes helped teams (and individuals) to take note of the journey — to record the struggles and the small weekly victories that led to the launch of a new product. Writing and sharing publicly helped people to reflect on what had happened that week. Weeknotes helped them to learn from the process, kept stakeholders up-to-date, and brought anyone else who was interested along for the ride.

But weeknotes aren't limited to digital teams. You can write them too.

Unlike a daily diary, weeknotes are normally written on a Friday or a Sunday. They're a review of the week: some noting down of events, some reflection, some gratitude. Whether you've learned something big or noticed something small, a weeknote is a good place to put it. As little or as much as you like, in paragraphs or bullet points.

The act of writing is helpful and doing it in public even more so. Regular writing, even for an audience of one, makes curiosity a habit, not a personality type. And publishing your weeknotes online holds you accountable. It makes you put that little more into it — and, when you're flagging, forces you to put something out into the world, just to keep face.

Writing can also help you see where the interesting patterns lie. Sometimes you'll realise things you thought were really important aren't quite the big deal you were expecting. And those small acts or quick things that seemed like nothing at the time were pivotal to the rest of the week.

It's likely you keep a calendar to remember the big things — the births, deaths, marriages, new jobs, home moves. Weeknotes can help you pay attention to and reflect on the small things, because sometimes that's where the most interesting things are hiding. After all, the small stuff is what novels, art, comedy and films are made of.

Try weeknotes. You could:

— **Write about your progress at work** — however you want to define it. You could write in public or on an internal forum, like your company intranet or wiki. You can even do it as an email to your team. A great format is just to answer these two questions: What did we do this week? What did we learn this week?

— **Write about the things you've seen or done** — you could write about your progress with a personal project, the plants in your garden, or the things you've noticed on your journey to the office. Weeknotes don't need to be grand.

— **Make the most of the format** — use your weeknotes for reflection or review. How did one day of the week compare to the next, or this week compare to last? What was different this month to last month? See if you can spot patterns over time. Alternatively, use your weeknotes to tell a story. Conveniently, every week has a beginning, a middle and an end: what was the story of the week?

More tips are available from blogger Giles Turnbull: see *gilest.org/weeknotes-tips*

DO 26
Weeknote!

Making on the internet

One of the joys of the internet has been the way it's become easy to get stuff made. Once upon a time it was a struggle to make your own book or get badges printed or what-have-you. Now it's just some clicks away.

Newspaper Club is a great example. They make it easy for you to publish your own newspaper. And Anne Ward, their CEO, also happens to be an expert in exactly this kind of interest-led self-publishing. She writes and publishes absolutely gorgeous photobooks (see page 128).

I asked her to tell us about it.

I used to blog, and share photos on social media. The blog lapsed after a while. I didn't feel like writing, but not sharing my photos created a sort of mental logjam, where the burgeoning collection of photos that weren't going anywhere began to stress me out.

I'm not sure if being a librarian made me this way, but my happy path is collecting > classifying > ordering > sharing. I don't feel right until the photos have been 'freed' into the world. So doing books or putting stuff online isn't so much about showing everyone my genius, more a kind of physical urge to free up headspace for new things.

When online sharing began to drift, I became more interested in making physical mementos from my photos. For years I made my kids a book of photos every Christmas that documented where they'd been, what they were into, etc. I really enjoyed the process of this, of pinning something down and making it more permanent.

A lot of the things I'm interested in are fleeting, or going out of fashion — relics from the past — so 'collecting' them by taking photos means they can live on after they have physically gone.

Two things drove the photobooks, like a sort of push and pull. The push was the urge to let air into the 'archive' of photos that was floating about on hard disks, etc. The pull was a picture of what I wanted the photobooks to be like — little worlds — based on old postcard books and tourism booklets that I've collected. That determined the format of A5, one photo per page, no captions, and the heft of making a small (but weighty!) book rather than a newspaper or zine.

The first book I worked on was about signs. When it came to sequencing 60 photos, I realised I didn't really know where to start, but I was inspired by a photographer called Iain Sarjeant whose photobooks have a similar format. His photos always work well in pairs, so instead of having to worry about all 60 photos, I just looked for pairs of photos that had something (subject, colour, shape, vibe) in common.

Once I'd got the hang of the sequencing, I tried it out and ended up doing 'Beside the Seaside' first. I really enjoyed this, as it was a chance to create a little world full of super-condensed seaside vibes. I like being able to highlight what's interesting (to me) and build it into a collection that hopefully works as an antidote to all the grimness and negativity in the world.

 DO 27

You can make your own photobooks via various online services. Build a world like Anne does — super-condensed vibes.

Sheer Art Attack

My friend Ben and I once used the internet to do 'art'.

We had an idea to do one of those half-and-half scarves you can buy at football matches. One half Liverpool, one half Manchester United. Real fans hate them, which makes them interesting. We thought they'd be a good thing to turn into art so we found a website that made them and designed some scarves out of famous art feuds.

Then we entered them into the Royal Academy's Summer Exhibition.

We didn't have much hope of getting in; if we hadn't we'd have blogged about it and that would have been part of the fun.

But we were very lucky. Grayson Perry was the head of the judges and he likes an art joke, so we got in.

A friend of mine told me he thought the scarves were the worst thing in the exhibition.

We've tried again every year since (though Ben has made considerably more of the effort than me) and not got in. It adds some rhythm to the year and makes us feel like artists.

At the other end of the scale, I always try and send postcards to The Secret Postcard Show at a lovely little gallery called The Old Lockup in Cromford, Derbyshire (see over).

I normally make collages out of headlines from the *Derby Telegraph*. That seems appropriate. Secret postcard shows happen at galleries all over the country, usually as fundraisers, and anyone can send in their art.

The point, for you, is not to do something brilliant. The point is to get used to sharing. That's the hard bit.

 DO 28

Support your local art gallery. Enter their secret postcard show. Or if art's not your thing, what about a writing competition? There are loads of them too and they have the same effect — they give you a goal and constraints and the possibility of recognition.

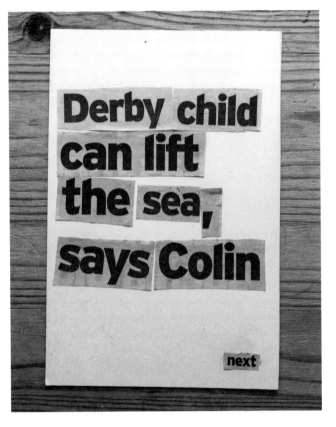

Constraints make you interesting

If you're a jacket nerd, you'll know about the company Paynter.

They make marvellous jackets. And also a little embroidered patch that reads 'Constraints Make You Interesting'.

That was bound to catch my eye.

It stems from their business model. They've decided to make jackets with the absolute minimum of waste, so they won't make one until someone's ordered it. Which means they only do limited runs and they only do them four times a year.

So, they have to think harder than most companies about how to get things done.

Part of their inspiration was Dr Seuss. He wrote *Green Eggs and Ham* only using 50 words after making a bet with a friend. It sold 8 million copies.*

Huw from Paynter told me:

If a story didn't have any constraints, or hurdles, or ups and downs, it'd be a bit boring. Putting a constraint on yourself means you're in a slightly harder, more interesting place.

The first shoot we did was on an iPhone. That was a constraint of having no money. And we asked a few friends to model for us but it turned shoots into something with a genuine and honest vibe. And that comes across in the photography. If you had proper models there, they probably wouldn't help you set up the white backdrop or carry it across a beach or carry loads of heavy stuff across a mountain. For them it'd be work, whereas for us it's making memories.

It's easy to convince yourself you don't have the right conditions to do your project. But you almost certainly have the right conditions to do *something*. And that thing might well be better. As the patch says, constraints make you interesting.

* And that's why Catrinel Tromp, a psychologist at Rider University, called her theory about the way constraints make us more creative the *Green Eggs and Ham Hypothesis*.

● **DO 29**

Pick a project you've always meant to do — or you're right in the middle of — but which you find too daunting. Put enormous constraints around it. Like only giving yourself 20 minutes. Do it now.

Formats make it easy

One way of imposing a constraint is to follow a format.

Things like 'seasons' and 'series' are great ways of framing your output. They're bigger than a single episode but they're completable. Sitcoms are 26 minutes. TV dramas are eight episodes. World Cups are every four years (until the monsters at FIFA have their way). These formats impose form, they are constraints, but they also create boundaries. They make things finishable.

I first saw this done by the newsletterer Dan Hon. He framed bursts of newsletters as 'seasons' — with names and numbers — which gave each burst some sense of coherence but also gave him permission to stop.

We're not surprised and let down when a series of our favourite TV programme finishes. We get excited by the last episode and start waiting for the new season to start. Which might be years away. You can apply that kind of framing to all sorts of things.

● DO 30
Create a 'limited edition' version of something you're making. Give it a name. Finish it.

Shorter stories

Here's a great example of using a constraint and inventing a format from Anne.

Remember the first lockdown, those warm spring days, when we lucky folk, those of us not sick, or caring for the sick, working from home and still being paid, built our days around an hour's exercise and what we might have for dinner? Instagram was full of people teaching themselves to bake bread or knit or juggle. I learned nothing and failed to use that time for any kind of enrichment activity. Then, when it was clear to everyone except our leaders that a second wave was coming and no one was going home for Christmas, things seemed darker, more awful.

At that point, I started writing some tiny stories. Taking the number of days in the month, I produced 30 stories of 30 words, an attempt to chronicle the times. This was the first:

'Remember when the *Daily Mail* had never heard of virologists?'

'And you said that going to a virology conference in Klosters was skiing on the rates?'

'I miss those days.'

Oddly, this was an actual conversation I'd had years ago with two friends of mine, one of whom is a virologist and was going to a conference in Switzerland, paid for by her institution. Of course, that was before we knew that she was going to save our lives, when we could still poke fun at whatever she did in her laboratory and white coat. But I'd actually made a note of it in my notebook: 'Things that might make a short story'. Lucky.

Ideas for the meat of the stories were never a problem. It turned out that, like most of us, I had more than 30 things to say about the pandemic. So much so that I did it all again in January 2021, perhaps the bleakest point of the whole nightmare, and again in November 2021, a year later. I talked about students missing out on life, children bursting school bubbles, Khalid mourning the football. I wrote about tiers, about old people dressing up to get their first dose of Pfizer, taking a walk with one other person, calling into radio talk shows and, of course, life on Zoom.

Seeing herself on the Zoom call, Pam examines her hair.

'I look like the blond guy in Spinal Tap,' she thinks. It's a difficult moment.

'I need to start bothering.'

Some of these things happened to me. Others I imagined or stole from other people's lives. Once I'd started, there was so much to say, which was why the self-imposed word limit was a boon. Crafting an idea down and down was a good creative challenge. And setting the boundary of a month at a time put a larger structure in place. It also meant that, a year later, writing 30×30 in the strange half-and-half world of November 2021 made me review things I had written 12 months earlier.

Brian stares at his annual appraisal form. Can it really be 12 months since the last time? Outline three achievements. Not dying. Not losing my mind. There is no third.

The good thing about a small writing task is just that, it's small, for the writer but also for the reader.

I shared my little tales on social media and my own blog. People seemed to like them. I think they resonated.

I produced little pamphlets of the stories, illustrated by my friend, Courtney Jones. Her drawings were completely right and, while travel was still impossible, queuing at the Post Office to send the booklets round the world was a joy.

None of this became a publishing phenomenon. I was not interviewed on Woman's Hour or picked up by a podcaster, but that was fine. I had created something small, for myself and those around me. Since then, I have written 21×21 for my son's 21st birthday. After an exhausting year for the world, I wrote one story for Ukraine and 24×24 for Advent 2022; again, my way to record and share a particular time.

Amir watches the news. From Kharkiv to Hackney, everyone is freezing. It's 2022, ffs. We were promised jet packs; now there's not even heating.

None of this is clever or unique. I haven't invented anything new but it's fun to do and to know I can do it again. Which I will, come the next communal bit of chaos.

 DO 31
Invent or borrow a format. Make three episodes.

You've been framed

Another way to make life easier when sharing is to think about the frame.

There's a magnificent clip that flies around TikTok of the late designer Virgil Abloh talking about a battered metal candle in a tin can that he's holding up to the camera.

He says:

If I put this candle in an all white gallery space it looks like a piece of art. If I put it in a garage it looks like a piece of trash, like someone would throw it away. It's dented. And I often use this analogy in design. I could either design the candle, spend a lot of time telling about the candle, or I can design the room it sits in.

The software engineer Alice Bartlett is a genius with frames. Her daughter once wanted to replicate an art show she'd seen. Alice elevated her daughter's work beyond the stuff that only a parent could love by thinking about the framing. She used square paper so lots of pictures could be stuck on the wall in an appealing grid. And she made mini artist bios and even red dots to make it look more real (see page 132).

We could send letters

Doing all this stuff just for yourself and never showing it to another soul is absolutely fine.

You'd get a lot out of it. It'd be interesting. But it'll be considerably more interesting if you share it with other people.

Being a bit of an introvert, I sometimes wish that wasn't true. But it is. At the heart of interestingness, somewhere, is entanglement with another brain.

When I first started telling people How To Be Interesting, I'd just say, 'Start a blog,' and that was pretty straightforward advice. But the internet was a lot smaller then and there weren't really trolls, influencers, monetisation and side-hustles.

It was easier, less fraught and more naive. I was also blithely unthinking about the amount of privilege I was bringing to that suggestion. It was easy for me to say.

I still think it's good advice, but there are more reasons now to be wary of oversharing on the internet. And even the most put-it-all-out-there person needs to be thoughtful about what they make public.

— **You can be anonymous, that's fine.** In some ways it's more interesting. Or you can create an alter ego. Just don't do that to be creepy, obvs.

— **You don't have to share yourself to share your ideas.** In fact, it's often more interesting if you don't talk about yourself. The best talks at the Interesting conference are the ones where people reveal some tiny thing about themselves while actually talking about something they're interested in, like gardening or Lego. Their sharing is oblique. Mystery is more interesting than obviousness.

— **And you don't have to post pictures of yourself either.** You can share your ideas without sharing your face.

— **You don't need to be everywhere.** You don't need all the socials. You can just pick a suitable channel for a project. And you can stop. You can delete it and shut it down. The interesting bit should be doing it, not what gets left behind.

— **You don't have to go *out* out.** You don't have to be accessible to everyone. You're after feedback, other minds paying attention. That could be friends and family on a private account, a discreet corner of the internet. You can start there at least. Baby steps.

— **And it doesn't need to be the internet.** You could send letters. Or postcards. Or publish pamphlets and sell them in the parish hall. Or paint on walls.

● **DO 32**
Create a social media account as a place for a project. Don't share anything personal, use it as a place to share something you're making. See how it feels.

Out out

'But I don't like meeting new people!'

I understand. I hate it too.

Events, gatherings, conferences, spontaneous social occasions. They can all be absolutely excruciating.

And, honestly, you don't have to go to them. It's perfectly possible to live an interesting and rewarding life on the internet. Or with a few close friends. Or in your own head.

But, if you're up for going out, there's a useful and compounding effect to the exchange of ideas with other people who are in the same room as you. And if you want to dial up your interestingness, finding ways to get people together, or to get together with people, is likely to help.

If you're one of life's natural hosts, you probably won't need this next section. You'll already be on the phone to a dozen people, inviting them round for a book club and fondue.

This is for that most delicate group of people, the introverts who want to chat.

Eventing

If you're nervous about events, it's often because of their unpredictability. Will you know someone there? When's a good time to arrive? Will I be expected to do something?

The best way out of this is to organise your own. These problems disappear. Other problems arrive but we'll solve them below.

The rules

People like events with explicit rules, otherwise they worry about the hidden rules they may not know, the etiquette and snobbery.

Priya Parker has written a brilliant book about this stuff called *The Art of Gathering* and she talks about the joy of 'pop-up rules'.

Arbitrary things you might invent, like:

— You must wear white
— Don't talk about 'what you do'
— You can't pour your own drink, someone else has to do it for you

As she says:

In the explicitness and oftentimes the whimsy of these rules was a hint of what they were really about: replacing the passive-aggressive, exclusionary, glacially conservative commandments of etiquette with something more experimental and democratic.

Rules also make your event feel like 'a thing' and that is half the battle. If you give an event a name (even something as boring as Coffee Morning), make it regular and invent some rules, it will become 'a thing'.

Badges help too. And stickers. You can get them made online and they're not too expensive.

The excuse

If you haven't got a thing, you need an excuse. Most social occasions are just chats around an excuse.

If you ask people to come over to your house and talk, they'll think you're strange.

If you say it's for a dinner party or poker or Grand Theft Auto, they're perfectly happy.

If you ask people to walk very slowly around a park full of holes, they won't; if you say it's golf, they might.

The great thing with these kinds of excuses is that they fill up the lull in the chat. As a last resort at a book club you can talk about the book.

And presentations are a great excuse.

My favourite phenomenon to emerge from lockdown was the PowerPoint Party. Friends or family getting together to do presentations at each other about the stupid and fun things that are the conversational grist of real life. Things like:

— 'Finland doesn't exist'
— 'How to get a boyfriend'
— 'Why pretzels are just confused bagels'
— 'Why Dora is the worst explorer'

You can watch these parties unfold on YouTube or TikTok. They're joyous and hilarious. They remind me of the anthropologist Polly Wiessner's work on the way gathering around a fire created cultures of story-telling among early humans.

Body language is dimmed by firelight and awareness of self and others is reduced. Facial expressions — flickering with the flames — are either softened, or in the case of fear or anguish, accentuated. Agendas of the day are dropped while small children fall asleep in the laps of kin. Whereas time structures interactions by day because of economic exigencies, by night social interactions structure time and often continue until relationships are right.

Being gathered round a PowerPoint presentation can have the same vibe.

The ceremony

I can't really remember how it started, probably just as a silly joke, but at the beginning of every Interesting conference we have a mass sing-along to 'The Final Countdown' by Europe.

I love watching the faces when it comes along. The new people are baffled and delighted at what's about to happen and people who've been before are reminded of this mad communal thing they did last time.

These little ceremonies and in-jokes all help to make an event feel special and outside the normal realm.

They make it personal.

 DO 33

Start an event. It could just be you and a friend meeting for a cuppa. But if you make a badge …

Putting it all to work

If you pick up some of these habits, you probably won't need advice on how to incorporate them into your job. You'll be having trouble keeping them out. But just in case, here are some ways to think about it.

You're building an analogy library

The poet Samuel Taylor Coleridge tells us in his diaries that he used to go to scientific lectures at the Royal Academy to 'renew my stock of metaphors'. That's a lot of what you're doing here.

The best presentations don't just tell people something — they tell them the same thing again and again but in different ways. They use analogies to help people understand. The point you want to make about the sales targets in Q4 will resonate more powerfully if it's accompanied by an interesting analogy. Same goes for that email you need to send.

You're showing you get it

A challenge for many in the modern workplace is working with 'the creatives': those people who are actually supposed to come up with the idea. They're very often intimidating and are treated as if they're a bit special. And they're often wary with people outside their professional domain. If you've got to work with them, it's massively useful to have a creative hinterland of your own — to demonstrate that you get what it's like putting your own work in public. They'll be easier to work with if they know you're used to taking a creative leap of your own.

You're getting used to working with ideas

One of the most awkward moments at work is when people who aren't used to it are suddenly asked to talk about 'ideas'. What do you think of this logo? What should our corporate principles be? What should we write on this flyer? These are hard things to talk about if you've not done it before. But now, of course, you're used to it. You've thought about what you like and why you like it. You're juggling with and collecting little creative thoughts on a dailyish basis. You're not intimidated by someone asking you to talk about colours for the new canteen.

Fin

The photographer Russell Duncan said it well:
'You are the secret weapon in any creative endeavour.'

Remember that Ursula Le Guin quote about making a virtue of your peculiarities? Or the Dolly Parton one about finding who you are and doing it on purpose? Listen to Russell, Ursula and Dolly.

If you are interested in the world, you'll get the world interested in you. By being you.

Good luck.

● **DO 34**
Have a go. Enjoy yourself.

Beside The Seaside   ANNE WARD

A Parade of Shops   ANNE WARD

Chips And Ice Cream   ANNE WARD

Sign Here   ANNE WARD

Resources

For more interestingness, visit:

The Art of Noticing *robwalker.substack.com*
Creative Inspiration *storythingsnewsletter.substack.com*
Dan Hon *newsletter.danhon.com*
Helen Lewis *helenlewis.substack.com*
Ingrid Burrington *buttondown.email/perfectsentences*
Jason Kottke *kottke.org*
Navaz Batliwalla *disneyrollergirl.net*
The Science of Creativity *anniemurphypaul.substack.com*
Why is this Interesting? *whyisthisinteresting.substack.com*
The Interesting Conferences *reasonablyinteresting.co.uk*

A wonderful directory of blogs. Like the old days:
ooh.directory

Additional writing: *russelldavies.com/blog*

And if you're a glutton for punishment, there is more at:
buttondown.email/russell and *@dointeresting* on Instagram.

About the author

Russell Davies is a writer, communicator and strategist. He's spent 30 years figuring out what happens when organisations and services meet the internet.

In his spare time, he's been a blogger, a columnist for *Wired*, he's made a BBC programme about the 'Internet of Things', he's organised the Interesting conferences and written books about PowerPoint and great British cafés.

His 'art' has featured at the Museum of Modern Art in New York, the Royal Academy Summer Exhibition and the Old Lock Up Gallery, Cromford.

russelldavies.com

© Jim Marsden / The DO Lectures

Thanks

None of the ideas in here are mine alone, they all came from reading, listening and conversation. Every book is a communal endeavour and it's weird that all that collective effort gets hidden in the acknowledgements. I think it's one reason more people don't try and write something like this. You should. You really don't have to do it all on your own.

These are the people I had those conversations with and I love them all. To start with, of course, Anne, Ben, Clem and Denise.

Anne says thanks to: Dad (and Mum, just to be fair, and not to suggest one parent is more interesting than another). Ben says thanks to: James Bridle, Mark Davies, Rama Gheerawo and John Sorrell. Clem says thanks to: Simón, Seb, Dad and Mum. Denise says thanks to: Mum and Dad, for showing me the benefits of a good walk and saying hello to the people you meet on the way.

And big, big thanks to James Bridle who's peppered throughout this book and gave his time and thoughts incredibly generously.

Then there are the ongoing and lovely conversions with the various communities of THFT, Bulbasaurs and Interesting. Special thanks to anyone who's ever been to the Interesting conference or spoken there. And huge thanks to everyone who I talked to for and about this book, apologies if your bit didn't make the final version.

And, of course, big love to Miranda, Jess, Wilf and Dave at DO.

Edith Murray (b. 2018)
Angry ghost 2022
Chalk pen on Origami paper

Edith Murray (b. 2018)
Dog and bone 2022
Chalk pen on Origami paper

Edith Murray (b. 2018)
Seagull 2022
Chalk pen on Origami paper

Edith Murray (b. 2018)
Frog and tree 2022
Chalk pen on Origami paper

Edith Murray (b. 2018)
Flamingo 2022
Chalk pen on Origami paper

Edith Murray (b. 2018)
Fish 2022
Chalk pen on Origami paper

Edith Murray (b. 2018)
Giraffe 2022
Chalk pen on Origami paper

Edith Murray (b. 2018)
Mummy and Edith 2022
Chalk pen on Origami paper

Edith Murray (b. 2018)
FAST
Chalk pen on Origami paper

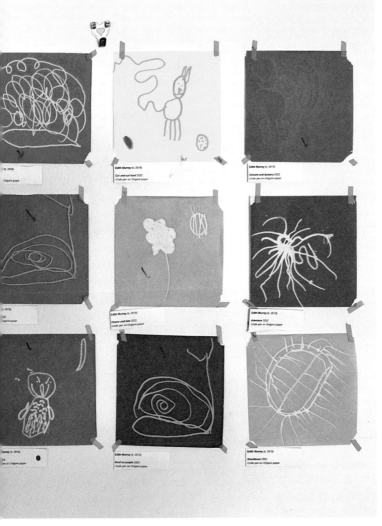

Books in the series

Do Agile Tim Drake

Do Beekeeping Orren Fox

Do Birth Caroline Flint

Do Bitcoin Angelo Morgan-Somers

Do Breathe
Michael Townsend Williams

Do Build Alan Moore

Do Deal
Richard Hoare & Andrew Gummer

Do Death Amanda Blainey

Do Design Alan Moore

Do Disrupt Mark Shayler

Do Drama Lucy Gannon

Do Earth Tamsin Omond

Do Fly Gavin Strange

Do Grow Alice Holden

Do Hope Gail Muller

Do Improvise Robert Poynton

Do Inhabit Sue Fan & Danielle Quigley

Do Interesting Russell Davies

Do Lead Les McKeown

Do Listen Bobette Buster

Do Make James Otter

Do Open David Hieatt

Do Pause Robert Poynton

Do Photo Andrew Paynter

Do Present Mark Shayler

Do Preserve
Anja Dunk, Jen Goss & Mimi Beaven

Do Protect Johnathan Rees

Do Purpose David Hieatt

Do Scale Les McKeown

Do Sea Salt
Alison, David & Jess Lea-Wilson

Do Sing James Sills

Do Sourdough Andrew Whitley

Do Start Dan Kieran

Do Story Bobette Buster

Do Team Charlie Gladstone

Do Walk Libby DeLana

Do Wild Baking Tom Herbert

Also available

The Book of Do A manual for living **edited by Miranda West**

Path A short story about reciprocity **Louisa Thomsen Brits**

The Skimming Stone A short story about courage **Dominic Wilcox**

Stay Curious How we created a world class event in a cowshed **Clare Hieatt**

The Path of a Doer A simple tale of how to get things done **David Hieatt**

Available in print, digital and audio formats from booksellers or via our website: **thedobook.co**

To hear about events and forthcoming titles, find us on social media **@dobookco**, or subscribe to our newsletter